CW01302970

Claudio Patrini

THE ESSENCE OF ZEN

The Path of Direct Insight

© 2023 Claudio Patrini

All rights reserved

Contents

Introduction 9

The Unique Reality 11

The Search Must Be Turned Inward 13

The Discriminating Mind 14

Beyond Intellect 15

The World of the Senses 17

The Flow of Sensitive Phenomena 18

Overcoming the Self 19

Our Universal Nature 21

Zen Is Not in Words 22

Truth Cannot Be Transmitted 23

The Barrier of Dualism 24

The Inadequacy of Words and Concepts 26

The Truth Cannot Be Grasped 27

We Are Already in the Truth 29

Access to Truth is Free 31

That Which Is Small 32

Not Gradualism, but Immediate Realization 33

It Is Not a Matter of Focusing and Meditating 34

Non-Dualism Is to Be Realized 36

Do Not Separate Spirit and Matter 37

Separations Are Generated by the Mind 38

Lighten the Weights 39

Not Denying the Mind, Not Submitting to the Mind 40

Activism Is the Work of the Self 41

Like a Mirror ... 42
We Should Not Add, but Take Away ... 43
The Way ... 44
The World of the Senses Is Neither to Be Accepted nor Denied ... 45
In Being, Everyone Has Unlimited Possibilities ... 46
The Proper Use of Words ... 47
We Must Not Identify with Individual Characteristics ... 49
Calm Is Within the Movement ... 50
Staying in What Is ... 52
Preferences, Even in the Search for Truth ... 53
Our Intimate Connection with Truth ... 54
Between Emptiness and Multiplicity ... 55
Pleasure and Pain, Two Faces of Being ... 57
The Sword of Zen ... 58
The Tide of Concepts ... 59
Bringing Multiplicity Back to the One ... 60
The Gifts of Suffering ... 61
Attachment to Insights ... 62
Simplicity ... 63
Imagined Spiritual Progress ... 64
In Order Not to Wander Aimlessly ... 65
One Cannot "Seek" the Way ... 66
True Knowledge Is Creative ... 68
Starting from Sensitive Experience ... 69
The Illusory Value of Ideals ... 71
Time ... 72
Space ... 74

Beauty of Nature and Attachment ... 76
We Know the World by Creating It ... 77
Denying All Representations of the Mind ... 79
Ordinary Man Is Already Perfect ... 80
Awakening from the Dream ... 81
Filled with Being ... 82
Zen Must Not Be Reduced into Concepts ... 83
Acknowledging the Miracle of Being ... 84
Change Is Only Apparent ... 85
Stop ... 86
Daily Commitment ... 87
True Zen ... 88
Alone or in Community ... 89
Zen Community ... 90
Subject and Object ... 91
Sacredness Is Everywhere ... 92
Listening with the Eyes ... 93
The Impossible Challenge ... 94
Zen Is Not a Philosophy ... 95
The Blows of the Masters ... 96
Advance and Retreat ... 98
Many Schools, One Zen ... 99
The Greatness of the Masters ... 100
Misunderstanding Teaching ... 101
The Language of the Masters ... 102
Koans ... 103
Our Real "Body" ... 104

Every Product of the Mind Is Deceptive 105

Don't Tell All 106

Objects Are Better Than Concepts 107

Honesty in the Search 108

Seeking One's Identity in Others 109

Life Itself Is the Way 110

Know Thyself 111

Inappropriate Eccentricities 112

Too Much Study 113

Zen Knowledge 114

Fallout 115

Zen Should Always Be Regenerated 116

Truth Is Before Words 117

The Wisdom Beyond Consciousness 118

The Moral Equivocation 119

The Deepest Compassion 120

Using the Senses, but Not to Take Advantage of Them 121

Do Not Start from the Assumption of Imperfection 122

Backward Path 123

No Attachment 124

Determinism and Freedom 126

So That Life Is Not Useless 127

The False Teachers 128

Enemies Are a Gift 129

When Teachers Seem to Lean on the Sensitive World 130

Zen "Thieves" 131

Outside and Inside 132

The Experience of Being	133
Riding the Tiger	134
Blind	135
Only Ourselves Can Free Ourselves	136
Meet Directly	137
The Iron Yoke	138
Fools Who Can See	139
Thought Is Not a Danger	140
Birth and Death	141
Don't Look for What Is Already in You	142
To Cling to Being Is to Lose It	143
Empty Substantiality	145
Not Only Knowledge	146
Simultaneously	147
Hit by the Arrow	148
The Subtle Feeling	149
Don't Look for a "Cake"	150
Understanding the Precepts	151
The Role of the Master	152
New Paths	154
From Great Distances	155
Finite and Infinite	156
Enlightenment Has No Cause	157
From Slaves to Lords	158
Rebirth	159
The End of the Search	160
Before the World Appears	161

No One Can Become Enlightened 162

Compass 163

The Destination 164

Introduction

After Gautama Buddha conducted his preaching around the fifth century B.C.E., numerous philosophies, religious practices and precepts derived from his teaching were accumulated over time, in addition to various collections of his discourses. The Buddha's message became increasingly standardized and ritualized, and covered with a multiplicity of concepts.

A current of Buddhism that developed in China around the 6th century CE, and which took the name Ch'an, succeeded in ridding Buddhism of all the superstructures that had tarnished its original meaning. Ch'an, later spreading to Japan as well, took the name Zen; but it is in its early Chinese development that we must look for the elements of Zen's originality and extraordinary depth.

Zen teaches us to see the world, and ourselves, without the mediation of concepts and emotional filters. It brings us to know our true nature, beyond the psychological characteristics and personal history with which we usually identify.

The behavior and words of the ancient Zen masters often appear enigmatic and provocative. But the purpose of the masters was not to display cunning and extravagance, but to guide people out of the narrows of the mind and into the open space of freedom.

If in the words of the ancient Zen masters we can sense the signs of genuine adherence to reality, we recognize that those words were spoken *for* us, and that they were spoken *by* us.

The Unique Reality

The senses and conceptual thinking lead us to believe that reality is composed of a multiplicity of objects. Zen reveals that this world of separation is only apparent, and that it is possible to come to recognize, at its base, being, which is the realm of freedom.

"Essence manifests internally as a log or rock, because it remains motionless and unchanged; externally, it manifests as space, in which there are no obstacles or constraints." (Huang Po: Treatise on the Transmission of Mind).

To know being is to overcome all distinctions, including that between the human and the divine. Indeed, the divine, the Buddha, cannot subsist as a separate entity, but only as the living essence of all that exists.

Thought, which by its nature makes distinctions, cannot be the proper means of recognizing the unity of the whole.

"There is no reality other than the One Mind, and both the Buddha and sentient beings originate from it. [...] As soon as we try to grasp it with thought, it escapes." (Huang Po: Treatise on the Transmission of Mind).

"One Reality contains all realities. One moon is reflected in all waters, and all the moons of all waters are united in that moon." (Yung-Chia Ta-Shih: Song of Enlightenment).

The Search Must Be Turned Inward

No truth matters unless it is based on knowledge of being, which can only take place in the depths of oneself.

Directing cognitive activity toward what is external, using external cognitive tools (such as ideas transmitted by others), and generally chasing the senses and concepts are all actions that lead us away from truth.

"If we look for Mind externally, in the world of forms, it moves away from us." (Huang Po: Treatise on the Transmission of Mind).

"It is not birth and death that I have to deal with [...]. Let us devote ourselves only to the root, without attending to the branches." (Yung-Chia Ta-Shih: Song of Enlightenment).

"Do not tend another's bow, do not ride another's horse, do not speak of another's mistakes, do not inquire into another's business." (The Door Without a Door).

The Discriminating Mind

Zen truth is not knowable through discriminating thought, that is, through what are considered the normal modes of cognition.

The starting point for following Zen is therefore to distance oneself sharply from knowledge that is the result of discriminating consciousness: truth has nothing to do with such "knowledge," and it decisively repudiates it.

"When a common man realizes this, he is a sage. If a wise man understands it, he is but a common man." (The Door Without a Door).

Even the truths of Buddhism and one's personal essence, when viewed through the lens of discriminating consciousness, become errors and obstacles on the path to truth, and it is preferable to disavow them.

"Emperor Wu of Liang asked Master Bodhidharma: 'What is the main meaning of the holy teachings?' Bodhidharma replied, 'Empty, without holiness.'" (The Blue Cliff Record).

Beyond Intellect

To know the immensity of being, the reductive concepts of the intellect are totally inadequate. There is, however, another kind of knowledge, which we can bring out when we take away from the intellect that precedence it is not entitled to.

"The elephant does not take the rabbit's way, the Great Enlightenment is beyond the narrow limits of the intellect. Stop measuring the sky with a reed." (Yung-Chia Ta-Shih: Song of Enlightenment).

"Nan Ch'uan said, 'Mind is not the Buddha, knowledge is not the Way.'" (The Door Without a Door).

Reality is a single whole, the parts of which are inextricably connected. The mind, by distinguishing individual parts and producing one-sided judgments about them, completely fails in the task of grasping reality as a whole.

"The Way is not difficult, it only requires not having preferences." (Seng-ts'an: Poem of Deep Faith).

The mind's evaluations pollute reality, contaminate it and corrupt its taste and beauty.

"Sand in the rice, thorns in the mud." (The door without a door).

There are no distinctions in being: nothing is excluded from it, just as there are no parts of the sky that are not irradiated by sunlight, nor parts of the earth that are not bathed by rain.

"With clear skies, the sun radiates brightly; when the rain falls, the earth becomes moist." (The Door Without a Door).

The World of the Senses

The world of the senses attracts us by stimulating our curiosity with ever new and strange forms, making us imagine that we can find extraordinary situations and objects in it that will fill us with wonder and pleasure. In this way we end up constantly wandering in the sensible world and in the illusion of time and space.

For Zen, in this way we are "losing life," because we waste the opportunity to discover ultimate reality and to be born to true life.

The paths of the physical world, even when they are flat and easy, are never free from suffering, and above all they do not lead to any real goal.

We must always be clear that the one and only true path worth taking is the transcendent one, which overcomes all limitations and reconnects us to being.

The Flow of Sensitive Phenomena

Reality manifests itself in a stream of sensible data, mingling and transforming, in a free and incessant dance. The discriminating mind, through what in Zen is called "sixth consciousness," filters this dance with its categories, establishes boundaries, fixes constants, identifies separate objects, ascribes causal links. But the enlightened, like infants, know how to see, beyond the limitations of the mind, the living flow of reality, in which there is no subject and object, and no inner world separate from an outer world.

"A monk asked Chao Chou, 'Does an infant possess the sixth consciousness?' Chao Chou replied, 'Throw a ball into the swift current.'" (The Blue Cliff Record).

Overcoming the Self

If we rely on the discriminating mind, the first consequence will be to experience the separation between us and the world, between "I" and "not-I."

Those who are subject to the illusion of being an individual relate everything to themselves, claim reasons and rights and create conflicts. On the other hand, when we are capable of not being dominated by the sense of "I," we access enormous power, and everything becomes possible because the limits of causal and space-time mental structures are overcome.

"If your self is clear and everything is self, when you go to a teacher you do not see a teacher; when you search in yourself you do not see that you have a self. [...] You don't neglect your daily tasks, yet you don't feel proprietary about anything." (Teachings of Master Fo-yen).

Those who remain bound to the belief that they are in individual, cannot get out of the dualistic world produced by the mind, and cannot access the truth. To become "dragons" one must "go up the current of a waterfall," one must go against common sense. The experience of truth presupposes that we discover a depth in ourselves that is incomparable to the mind-generated sense of self.

"If you have never known him personally, it is as if he is many worlds away." (The Blue Cliff Record).

Truth cannot be found in the "dead waters" of the discriminating mind.

"At the Dragon Gates in three rows, where the waves are high, fish become dragons, but fools continue to fish in the evening pond." (The Blue Cliff Record).

What the unenlightened man considers most valuable is his own self. The attachment to the ego is subtle and insidious: even when one considers oneself poor and humble, one is only feeding the sense of the ego.

Zen presupposes a true and total abandonment of ego-attachment, and a total willingness to unhesitatingly put one's beliefs on the line without thought of danger.

Our Universal Nature

We are not our physical body, we are not our thoughts and we are not what we normally, when we reflect on ourselves, refer to as "I." What we are is not something individual. In us we find the vastness of the whole universe, and the reconciliation of every division.

"The true nature of every man contains in emptiness all objects [...]; observing all beings exactly as they are, what is good and what is bad, it does not detach itself from them, nor is it defiled by them; it is like the emptiness of space." (Hui Neng: Platform Sutra).

"Light and darkness eliminate and prevail over each other, but space is a vast emptiness that is not changed by it. The same can be said of Mind, which is the essence of the Buddha and sentient beings." (Huang Po: Treatise on the Transmission of Mind).

"When you go deep within yourself, you will suddenly discover that everything you need is already there, perfect and in abundance, and that nothing is lacking. [...] You will realize that from the very beginning you have been a Buddha, nothing but a Buddha. Enlightenment will give you nothing but this truth." (Huang Po: Treatise on the Transmission of Mind).

Zen Is Not in Words

It is not by following many masters and listening to many talks that one will come closer to understanding Zen; those who seek only words will never find Zen. Words, at best, are the lifeless residue of the inspiration that generated them: feeding on words is like feeding on garbage.

Zen cannot be communicated with words, because it is not a doctrine, it is not something external and objectifiable; the meaning of Zen must spring from within each person, and is only achievable through the discovery of one's true self. This is why "there are no Zen masters."

"Huang Po said, 'I am not saying that there is no Ch'an, but that there are no Ch'an masters.'" (The Blue Cliff Record).

Truth Cannot Be Transmitted

Truth cannot be transmitted; if one tries to communicate it verbally, one falls into the trap inherent in the dualism of language, and truth is lost.

Although Zen has a tradition accumulated over centuries of history, any man who wants to understand Zen must start from scratch, retracing the difficulties and mistakes of all those who have gone before him. There are no shortcuts, no help can come from outside, because the truth intimately concerns each of us, and each of us must understand for himself.

Truth can only be *our* truth, because we are being, and being is each of us.

"The Patriarchs and Buddhas never taught men." (The Blue Cliff Record).

The Barrier of Dualism

Dualistic thinking is incapable of understanding truth; it kills life because it cannot grasp the whole.

We must avoid falling into the error of qualifying something as "positive" and desirable in an unambiguous way; for this means falling into the dualism and illusions of mental constructions.

A statement and its opposite, because of their unambiguity, will always be possible on any subject, and both will be true and false. It is necessary to be free from the judgments of the mind and from words.

If we look at reality through dualistic thinking, we will not see reality but separate and dead fragments.

One cannot understand the fundamental truth of Zen through reasoning. If we dwell on thinking, we have already lost the ability to grasp the moment when reality manifests itself in its immediacy.

"Flashes flashing, sparks shooting from a flint; the blink of an eye in a moment - and it is already is lost forever!" (The Door Without a Door).

For Zen, the purpose of existence is to find the One, and no price is too high to achieve this goal. To remain in the prison of dualistic thinking is to spend a useless and powerless life. By finding contact with reality, we also come to know our enormous power.

"Those who dispute between right and wrong are slaves to right and wrong." (The Door Without a Door).

The Inadequacy of Words and Concepts

Knowledge based on rationality and expressible in language returns only a dead and coarse simulacrum of reality. Authentic wisdom requires the recognition of a level of existence that cannot be "seen" by rational knowledge, because it is too subtle, spontaneous and vital to pass through the grid of concepts.

"Wu-tsu said, 'A buffalo passes through a window. Its head, horns, and four legs have passed. But why doesn't the tail pass?'" (The door without a door).

"Words and concepts: staying with them leads further and further off the road; staying away from them, you go wherever you want." (Seng-ts'an: Poem of Deep Faith).

It is not concepts that create life and move reality. Reality is simple and directly experienceable.
Multiplying discourses, explanations and distinctions only distances one from reality. To understand Zen, one must stop relying on discourses, and the dictates of the self.

The Truth Cannot Be Grasped

Truth cannot be "seen" as one sees an object on the outside: it is what, in us, sees, it is the act of seeing. If you try to objectify truth, you immediately end up with something static and dead, and thus with the exact opposite of truth, which is always a "becoming," a vital creation. What is objective is part of the dualistic world created by the mind. In the reality of being there are no "objects," because everything is "subject"; nothing is seen as external, static and objective, because everything is ourselves, everything lives in us and we are the life of the whole.

"You see it clearly - but to whom could you communicate it?" (The Blue Cliff Record).

"Nothing true can be found anywhere, because the true cannot be seen." (Hui Neng: Platform Sutra).

It is not possible to describe the truth; everyone has to discover it for himself, putting his life on the line. The basic indication that can be given is not to get lost by following words and the appearance of the senses: it would be like believing that the moon is always shaking, just because you are confusing it with its reflection on the waves.

"Remarkable! Observe how rough it is - the moon reflected on the waves." (The Blue Cliff Record).

Providing explanations about being only adds to the confusion. No one can claim knowledge about ultimate reality, because to speak of it is already to deny it. Zen masters considered themselves decidedly and proudly ignorant. Probably Socrates' phrase, "I know that I do not know," also alluded to this.

"Not even the ancient Buddhas said they had arrived there." (The Blue Cliff Record).

We Are Already in the Truth

There are no secrets. Truth is manifest around us, and it is always present, intimately connected to our true being.

We must discover truth by observing our true nature, that is, by looking within ourselves directly, without resorting to thoughts and judgments.

Being is our home, and it is only the deception of the mind that makes us believe we have strayed from it.

"You cannot describe it; you cannot paint it; you cannot praise it sufficiently; stop trying to grasp it with your head! There is no place where you can hide your original face; even when the world is destroyed, it is indestructible." (The Door Without a Door).

"A monk asked, 'How can I free myself?' Shih-t'ou replied, 'Who on earth imprisoned you?'" (Transmission of the lamp).

"Walking is Zen, sitting is Zen; speaking or being silent, moving or standing still, Being is always there, quiet." (Yung-Chia Ta-Shih: Song of Enlightenment).

"Ma-tsu said, 'All beings have never been outside the Truth; always dwelling in it, they eat and dress, speak and respond. [...] Return to the source with one thought, and your mind will be the very mind of the Buddha.'" (Sayings of the ancient personalities).

"Someone asked, 'What is the gateway to the truth of enlightenment?' Chao Chou replied, "The example of all times."" (The Sayings of Chao Chou).

"Truth does not need to be established, and the false never existed." (Yung-Chia Ta-Shih: Song of Enlightenment).

Access to Truth is Free

Reality is already open; there are no specific conditions for reaching it. When we see specific conditions, it is because we are in the domain of the mind, and not in the domain of truth.

"There are no particular paths to get there [...]. Buddhism has neither east nor west, neither south nor north." (Teachings of Master Fo-yen).

"The door of truth is without a door." (The door without a door).

Truth is not something external, which we must strive to seek: it is inherent in our being, and to find it, we need only find ourselves.

Any good that comes to us from the outside is worthless to us, because the source of all value lies in our inner activity. It is real and valuable only what we bring to life by making it flow from the depths of our being.

"It has been said that what comes through the door can never be your treasure. Whatever you obtain through external circumstances is destined to perish." (The door without a door).

That Which Is Small

In Zen, hierarchies of values constructed by the mind have no value: what appears large and powerful is no more important than what is tiny and fragile, and even the most vulnerable being is indispensable to the existence of the whole.

"Every coral branch supports the moon." (The Blue Cliff Record).

Zen knowledge enables one to free oneself from all mind-generated inequality and all pride associated with the illusion of individuality. In order to recognize the importance of what is small and humble, one must make oneself small and humble, that is, one must overcome the belief that one is an individual-and thus that one is, as an individual, at the center of the world.

Not Gradualism, but Immediate Realization

In Zen, one cannot be satisfied with partial and gradual achievements, and must always strive for what is beyond what the mind presents as possible and normal.

Zen does not require us to delve into long meditations, but to instantly grasp the unfathomable depth of reality. If we linger in the doubts of the mind, it is impossible for us to reach the truth. If we rely on the modes and characteristics of the finite world, constructed by the patterns of the mind, the infinite within us remains obscured.

Reality must be understood the instant it arises; if we dwell on reflection, reality is already lost. It is like the difference between the vitality of the falling rain compared with the water that has collected and lies dead in the pond after the rain has ceased.

It Is Not a Matter of Focusing and Meditating

Zen is not meant to calm the mind, and it has nothing to do with psychological or meditative techniques, because better emotional balance or the ability to detach oneself from thoughts and emotions are achievements that still remain within the sphere of the mind. Whether the mind is agitated or calm has no relevance, because the essential reality is on a level that transcends the mind.

True appeasement of the mind is achieved by realizing that the mind does not exist, and by ceasing to identify oneself with particular physical and psychological characteristics, seemingly linked in a temporal continuity. It is only the mind that makes us believe that we are those characteristics. Instead, it would be correct to say we are that which experiences those characteristics, and that in which those characteristics manifest.

Enlightenment does not occur as the result of a planned action, but is like being exposed to the sudden and unpredictable attack of something that threatens all our certainties and our very existence.

Identification with a physical body is perhaps what binds us most to the world of illusion; with enlightenment we discover that our essence resides in a dimension higher than the physical sphere, and of which the physical sphere is a manifestation.

Inevitably, to a world dominated by mental patterns, such knowledge will appear worthless.

"Because men have dulled minds, they seek awakening through formal exercises instead of devoting themselves to penetrating the true nature of their selves." (Hui Neng: Platform Sutra).

"Bodhidharma was sitting facing the wall. The Second Patriarch, standing in the snow, cut off his arm, presented it to Bodhidharma and said, 'My mind is still not at peace! I beg you, Master, pacify my mind!' Bodhidharma replied, 'Bring me your mind and I will pacify it'. 'I have sought my mind, but have never been able to grasp it,' said the Second Patriarch. Bodhidharma said, 'I have pacified your mind.'" (The door without a door).

"Ma-tsu said, 'The Sravaka [one who masters the practice of entering the state of deep concentration] has buried himself in the Void and does not know how to come out of his quiet contemplation because he does not know the Buddha nature.'" (Sayings of the ancient personalities).

"If you strive to achieve calmness by stopping movement, the calmness you achieve is still movement." (Seng-ts'an: Poem of Deep Faith).

"Those who do not understand that the Mind is the Buddha, and seek to achieve results through discipline related to form, expose themselves to wrong fantasies and leave the right path." (Huang Po: Treatise on the Transmission of Mind).

Non-Dualism Is to Be Realized

If we say that to access non-dualism we must avoid language, rational awareness, the search for causal connections and generally any activity of the discriminating mind, we still remain within the discursive mind that we would like to overcome: we are in fact expressing the concept of how to overcome concepts.

To access non-dualism, we must get in touch with our true nature, and from there make gestures (or even utter words) that express being. Therefore, a real, creative act of connecting with the One is needed. Merely thinking about non-dualism has no effect on knowledge and reality.

"By saying 'is,' no real thing is affirmed. By saying 'is not,' no real thing is denied." (The Blue Cliff Record).

If we remain at the level of conceptual thinking, even if we advocate non-dualism we will only deny it, perpetuating the deception of the mind.

"To deny reality is to affirm it, and to affirm emptiness is to deny it." (Seng-ts'an: Poem of Deep Faith).

Do Not Separate Spirit and Matter

The distinction between an earthly world, imperfect and impermanent, and a heavenly world, perfect and imperishable, is the work of the mind, and is a trap of disastrous consequences. If the search for truth starts from this basic distinction, it is doomed to failure.

Only by radically eliminating all mental constructions, including those concerning the superiority of Zen and the spiritual world, can we come to truly (and not only conceptually) recognize in what the greatness of being consists. For being is manifest everywhere, even in what to the mind are imperfections; and everything turns out to be connected, in the unity of being.

Separations Are Generated by the Mind

Dualism and separation are generated by the mind. If we know how to look at reality without filtering it with the categories of the mind, we find that there is no separation in it.

In being, there is no subject as opposed to an object, there is no "I" and "you," and there is no difference between man and God. Those who discover their true nature know that they are nothing, and they know that they are all that exists. To remain bound to the patterns of the mind leads to no knowledge, and has no effect on reality.

"Before you have penetrated, it is like a silver mountain, like an iron wall. When you have succeeded in penetrating, you discover that from the very beginning you yourself were the silver mountain, the iron wall." (The Blue Cliff Record).

"In the supreme realm of true reality, there is no 'I' or 'other'." (Seng-ts'an: Poem of Deep Faith).

Lighten the Weights

The teaching of Zen is meant to "lighten from weights." As long as we are prisoners of the mind, we have to constantly carry the enormous weights of all the beliefs, judgments and knowledge we have accumulated, which must be continually nurtured. The very belief of being a "person," in order to preserve itself, requires to be continually validated and strengthened.

Zen aims to free us from the weight of mental constructions, showing us that we can exist without it, and that without it we can experience our true nature and freedom of being.

Not Denying the Mind, Not Submitting to the Mind

The path of Zen has to do neither with letting the mind wander (getting lost in illusion) nor with stopping the mind (an unnatural attempt, hindering the normal flow of life).

One must let the mind do its work, which in the realm of the sensible world may be appropriate. But one must not get attached to the mind's judgments, which are always one-sided and ultimately unfounded.

If one does not become entangled in the judgments of the mind, one spontaneously dwells in being, and recognizes that everything arises from being and to being it constantly returns.

"Then in the four seas the waters are calm, the hundred rivers return to the ocean water." (The Blue Cliff Record).

Activism Is the Work of the Self

To access the truth, one must experience the autumn of illusions, when the tree of the self withers, and the leaves of attachments fall. Letting go of the illusion of being an individual corresponds to remaining exposed to the events of life without resistance.

Just as the sky allows the rain to pass through it without altering its nature because of it, so we may find that if we do not resist events, our nature is not altered by them.

It is the self that prompts us to resist situations we judge unfavorable and to alter the world to make it conform to what the mind deems right and pleasing. The action of those who experience Zen is not moved by the ego and the mind, but by the freedom of being.

"A monk asked Yun Men, 'What is it like when the tree withers and the leaves fall?' Yun Men replied, 'The body exposed in the golden wind.'" (The Blue Cliff Record).

"Someone asked, 'Of all things, which is the hardest?' Chao Chou replied, 'If it is cursing, you can curse me all day long. If it is spitting, you can spit out whole oceans.'" (The Sayings of Chao Chou).

Like a Mirror

To live according to truth means to be like a perfect mirror, reflecting exactly everything that presents itself, without altering it with one's own subjective characteristics. It means standing toward the world with an attitude of total openness: nothing is rejected, and everything is welcomed with equal willingness.

"A monk asked Chao Chou, 'What is Chao Chou?' Chao Chou replied, 'Eastern gate, western gate, southern gate, northern gate.'" (The Blue Cliff Record).

Zen teaches that one does not reach truth by following thought, nor does one reach it by trying to stop thought. Rather, one must remain in what is, like a highly polished mirror that reflects without interference every particular feature of everything that presents itself.

The Buddha, by his mere presence, could drop the veil of ignorance in those who observed him; for he who dwells in being expresses, for those who are receptive, the simplicity, humility and peace of being.

We Should Not Add, but Take Away

In order to achieve truth, we must not add something to what we are and do, instead we must take something away: we must let go of distinctions and preferences.

Language is the preferred vehicle for the emergence of distinctions and preferences because by its nature it can only describe a dualistic reality. It is therefore inevitable that, in order to explain Zen, words at some point must stop, to leave room for an understanding that language cannot convey: it is the understanding of what remains when sensory phenomena and mental patterns are left out.

The Way

Even through a thousand directions, the Way is unique and direct; it cannot be uniquely defined, it cannot be "known."

"Examining them with the eye of truth, it turns out that none of these ancient masters knows where the Way is." (The Door Without a Door).

Any supposed progress toward truth is an illusion: the boundless vastness of being renders meaningless the prospect of a gradual approach to it.

"Before a step is taken, the goal is reached; before the tongue is moved, the speech is finished. Although your steps take you further each time, there still remains the empty space that all encompasses." (The Door Without a Door).

Outward acts and words do not count; what is already achieved before a step is taken counts; what is already expressed before a word is spoken counts. The Way is achieved through an act of freedom, through jumping out of the box, by giving up clinging to the illusory certainties of the mind.

The World of the Senses Is Neither to Be Accepted nor Denied

The Zen way departs from pure acceptance of factual reality, but it also departs from pure denial of factual reality. One does not accept the sense world, but neither does one deny it.

"When adherence to factual reality and opposition to factual reality are intertwined, even the Buddhas and Patriarchs pray for their lives to be saved." (The Door Without a Door).

The solution to this apparent contradiction lies in finding within oneself the capacity for immediate and free inner motion. By recognizing ourselves in the unlimited creativity of being, we discover that the level of the senses and reason is only apparent, and that our true nature resides in the freedom of being.

In Being, Everyone Has Unlimited Possibilities

All differences in abilities, all roles, hierarchies, victories and defeats that seem to characterize the world, disappear when looked at from a higher perspective.

In being, there are no predetermined laws, inevitable consequences and unchangeable situations. Ultimate reality is the realm of freedom. Everything lives in being, and everything has equal importance, and unlimited possibilities. At the level of being, there are no differences in value, and nothing is impossible for anyone.

"One can awaken her [the girl sitting in meditation near the Buddha's seat], the other cannot. Both are free. Here the god mask, there the demon mask; even failure is beautiful." (The door without a door).

The Proper Use of Words

If we rely on words, for example by referring to sacred texts of the past, we are already moving away from the truth. The only valid way to use words is to make words a conduit between one's direct experience of reality and the transmission of that experience to others.

If, instead of taking as the basis for one's words a direct experience of being, one takes as the basis for words expressed by others, one remains completely within a circuit of concepts, and will only propagate illusion and confusion.

"A line is cast into the swift current, those who are eager for the bait will be caught. Open your mouth just a little, and your life will be lost." (The Door Without a Door).

Although words are an inadequate means of expressing truth, there is no question of opposing words. Those who dwell in being are able to convey the meaning of Zen through any means of expression.

Words are a problem if they are taken as a starting point; they are not a problem at all if they are used as an expository medium for meanings that have their origin not in words but in the lived reality of being.

In any case, the language of those who know being is well recognizable because it is always simple and direct.

"He does not use grand words; before he speaks, he has already revealed the Way. If you keep on chatting in a refined way, you will never find the Reality [...]. Now, putting aside language and talk, say a word!" (The Door Without a Door).

We Must Not Identify with Individual Characteristics

We must avoid the mistake of identifying ourselves with any of our multiple and variable states of consciousness. We are not our body, and we are none of the psychological aspects we experience from time to time. We are not even our personal history.

"We go from one wrapper to another, like a traveler staying in a hotel. But if you have not yet realized this, do not run blindly. When earth, water, fire, and air suddenly separate, you will be like a crab struggling in boiling water with its many claws and many legs. When this happens, do not say that I did not warn you!" (The door without a door).

We are that immortal part that "sees" the states of consciousness we experience, without being altered by them. In being, unity and multiplicity coexist and are mutually essential, in a way inexplicable to the mind.

"The moon above the clouds is always the same; valleys and mountains are different. All are blessed, all are blessed! Is it one? Is it two?" (The door without a door).

Calm Is Within the Movement

The experience of being is not achieved by denying the sense world and trying to stop thoughts and emotions; the ultimate reality must be discovered within the sense world, delving into it and observing its deep essence.

"Only those who are conscious understand what 'movement' means [...]; if you try to keep the mind without movement, the stillness you achieve is that of the one who is not conscious; if you aspire to what is truly still, the stillness is in the movement itself [...]; there can be no Buddhahood where there is no consciousness." (Hui Neng: Platform Sutra).

"Do not construct knowledge based on the senses and thoughts; but at the same time do not seek Mind away from the senses and thoughts, and do not try to grasp Truth by rejecting the senses and thoughts. [...] Mind must be found while the senses and thoughts are in action." (Huang Po: Treatise on the Transmission of Mind).

The sense world is not separate from being; rather, it is its manifestation. It is by moving within it that we can encounter being.

"Observe carefully the various forms of stillness, and know that the fundamental reality is still; by sensing this, you will understand the activity of Being." (Hui Neng: Platform Sutra).

The same sensitive experience that is a source of illusion can become a source of enlightenment.

"Good friends, passions are basically enlightenment. When your previous thought is clouded yours is an ordinary mind; but if your next thought is enlightened, you are a Buddha." (Hui Neng: Platform Sutra).

Staying in What Is

We understand being when we stop looking for something we imagine far away.

It is sufficient to remain in what is, in what we are experiencing in the present moment. If we do not wander with thought, we can participate in every moment in the miracle of being, which is inconceivable to the mind.

"To walk on the edge of a sword, to run on the crest of an ice floe; without steps, and without ladders, to climb the cliffs without hands." (The Door Without a Door).

Preferences, Even in the Search for Truth

In phenomenal appearance, commonly positive and negative aspects are distinguished, and preferences are generated.

Even in the field of truth-seeking, it might seem more "elevated" to prefer "spirit" to "matter," or "emptiness" to "objects." But this is to remain in illusion.

Zen has nothing to do with these distinctions or any other.

"But great emptiness does not achieve the essence of Zen. It is better to completely reject both emptiness and all things." (The Door Without a Door).

Our Intimate Connection with Truth

The "scientific" method and objectivity of knowledge are generally held in high regard. This appreciation is deserved, but it should not make us forget that, in essence, all true knowledge is based on a connection with our deepest essence.

"All arguments based on logic are not true arguments, because they have no connection with my inner Light. [...]. It, like space, has no limits [...]; it is by seeking it that you lose it [...]; the great gate of compassion is completely open and unhindered." (Yung-Chia Ta-Shih: Song of Enlightenment).

"From my youth I have sought enlightenment through study [...]; but diving into the ocean to count the grains of sand is a totally useless effort [...]; what is the use of amassing a treasure that is not mine?" (Yung-Chia Ta-Shih: Song of Enlightenment).

Between Emptiness and Multiplicity

Many understand that the world of multiplicity is unsatisfactory, unfounded and insufficient to provide the fullness to which man aspires. This leads to seeking a reality of an opposite nature, which has been given various names: God, Buddha, spirit, emptiness, etc.

But trying to isolate oneself in the "spiritual" world by avoiding "contamination" with thoughts and desires related to "matter," and denying the laws of the sensible world, does not resolve the sense of incompleteness.

"Don't chase the outer tangles, and don't dwell in the inner void." (Seng-ts'an: Poem of Deep Faith).

"The Void understood in a negative sense denies the world governed by causality; thus confusion and disorder reign, and this attracts evil. But we also attract evil when we attach ourselves to objects by denying emptiness." (Yung-Chia Ta-Shih: Song of Enlightenment).

The solution must be an intimate understanding of the vital interpenetration of the two polarities. Such an understanding shows that the supposed antithesis of emptiness and multiplicity does not exist except as a construction of the mind.

"The manifold exists because of the One, but do not attach yourself even to the One; if the mind is not disturbed, no harm comes from the ten thousand things." (Seng-ts'an: Poem of Deep Faith).

Pleasure and Pain, Two Faces of Being

The reality of being is not bound to fixed principles, but manifests freely in any condition.

It would be a mistake to want to address only what is pleasant and positive. Suffering is a manifestation of being on a par with pleasure, and is not to be denied or devalued.

Those who experience Zen know how to see, through both pleasure and pain, the wonder of being.

"Grand Master Ma was ill. The temple superintendent asked him, 'Master, how has your health been lately?' The Great Teacher said, 'Sun-faced Buddha, moon-faced Buddha.'" (The Blue Cliff Record).

The Sword of Zen

He who knows the truth possesses a sword that kills and gives life. For he can guide others to end the illusory life they were leading, and to discover the true life, which is free from the deceptive limitations of the mind. He kills the illusory life of the individual, and opens access to the free life of being.

"With a sharp sword in hand, one can kill or give life, depending on the occasion." (The Blue Cliff Record).

Jesus, too, had said, "I did not come to bring peace, but the sword." Freedom and peace cannot be established until after illusions and attachments have been defeated.

The Tide of Concepts

Since the truths of Zen are also expressed in words and concepts, some people make connections and deductions from these concepts and, on the basis of operations within the concepts, believe they can come to conclusions about reality. But if one detaches the concepts of Zen from the direct knowledge of being, from which they arose, they come to constitute an abstract and empty world, which has no connections or effects on reality.

Humans have long been accustomed to relating more to words and concepts than to reality. Occasional and purposeful use of the discursive mind is appropriate and useful in dealing with practical matters, but when we rely on the discursive mind so continuously that we come to identify with what should only be an occasional tool, we have before our eyes a filter that prevents us from distinguishing concepts from the direct experience of reality.

The tide of concepts is not to be taken lightly: while we believe we are using it at will to pursue our own ends, it is separating us from life.

"It is sorry to see those who joke with the tide: they will eventually fall into the tide and die." (The Blue Cliff Record).

Bringing Multiplicity Back to the One

Even in the face of the questions posed by the multiplicity that characterizes the world, it is necessary to know how to find an answer that leads back to the One.

It is a continuous challenge, it is a continuous invitation to confront the multiple in order to bring forth within oneself the truth of being, in which all apparent multiplicity is founded and manifests itself.

The Gifts of Suffering

The Way of Zen also passes through suffering. Suffering, like and more than other experiences, deserves that we deepen ourselves in it.

It is precisely by agreeing to be with whatever situations present themselves to us, without distancing ourselves from them with the comparisons, memories and predictions of the mind, that we can become intimate with reality, and grasp its deep nature. If we do this, it may happen that suddenly everything becomes clear to us, and we find ourselves free from the heavy and unnecessary burden of the sense of self.

Attachment to Insights

One danger in Zen is to have insights and to attach oneself to them by attributing immutable validity to them.

Insight sometimes makes it possible to grasp reality in its vital stage, before it is fixed by the mind into rigid, unchanging objects and meanings. However, when insights are petrified into concepts, the self is happy, because in concepts it does not feel challenged, and in them it can rest.

But one who lives Zen does not desire this kind of "rest"; he knows that reality is always new and elusive, and he is always careful to be found in tune with the vital momentum of being.

"The sitting, the leaning - stop thinking that these things happen to those who follow the Way of the Patriarchs!" (The Blue Cliff Record).

A similar warning was also expressed by Jesus: "The Son of Man has nowhere to lay his head."

Simplicity

The truth pointed out by Zen is simple. It is about abandoning complications, and opening up to the simple and immediate way in which reality comes to us.

Zen masters tried to guide to simplicity in various ways; in response to questions about Zen, they might, for example, point to an object, or make a quick gesture. The purpose was to teach how to grasp reality directly, with immediacy.

Everything we need is already contained in the simple everyday reality. The truth of Zen is not to be sought in a dimension beyond the world, but by deepening into the experience of the world.

Reality is so simple and directly available that this is precisely why we struggle to grasp it: the complications of the mind cause us to disregard simplicity.

"Precisely because it is extremely clear, it takes longer to understand it. If you realize that the flame of a candle is fire, you will find that the rice has already been cooked for a long time." (The Door Without a Door).

Imagined Spiritual Progress

Discriminating consciousness is not the true self. It wears "masks" and, changing with them the roles it plays, imagines itself to be changing and evolving: but this is not real spiritual progress.

It is essential to recognize that we are always inside the deception of subjective consciousness before we can really access our true nature and the dimension of being.

"Students of the Way do not realize truth because they remain bound to discriminating consciousness. It is the seed of birth and death, without end; fools mistake it for the true 'self'." (The Door Without a Door).

In Order Not to Wander Aimlessly

If we limit ourselves to the worldview constructed on the basis of sense perceptions organized by the mind, we continue to wander aimlessly. It is necessary to make up one's mind to take a leap and find one's true nature beyond the senses and intellect.

"Detach yourself from the four elements, and in Eternal Serenity eat or drink, at your discretion. When all relative things are revealed to be, in their essence, empty and passing, perfect enlightenment takes place." (Yung-Chia Ta-Shih: Song of Enlightenment).

One Cannot "Seek" the Way

The Way is not to be found outside ordinary experience, in supposed "metaphysical" dimensions.

But neither is the Way to be "sought," as if it were a goal to be achieved in the future. If we seek it, we move away from it, because we adhere even more closely to the ways of the discriminating mind and its concepts of cause-and-effect and space-time.

The Way must be discovered, realizing that it is broader and freer than the mind could ever imagine; in the boundless vastness of the Way, distinctions between right and wrong no longer make sense.

"Nan Ch'uan said, 'The Way does not belong to knowing or not knowing. To know is illusory; not to know is confusion. When without possibility of doubt you have really arrived at the true Way, you will find it as vast and unlimited as outer space. How can you speak, in it, of right and wrong?'" (The Door Without a Door).

In being, there are no separations, there are no "external" objects, everything is in us, and we are in everything. Dwelling in being, nothing is missing from us, and even the simplest and most natural events are precious sources of joy.

"Flowers in spring, the moon in autumn; breezes in summer, snow in winter. If your mind is not cluttered with useless things, you will live happy days." (The Door Without a Door).

True Knowledge Is Creative

In Zen, true knowledge cannot be merely limited to correct understanding; a true master must be able to creatively express the truth of Zen. His actions and words, getting rid of space-time conditioning, show that reality is unpredictable and "miraculous."

Only those who know full freedom know Zen.

One is not living Zen if one relies on beliefs, convictions and reasoning, because there is no life in them, and they are like wood that has already been burned. But one is not living Zen either if, while having a correct understanding of reality, one is not capable of transformative and revolutionary behavior.

Deep understanding of Zen brings with it the ability to operate actions that overthrow common sense and subvert what discriminating thinking considers the normal order of things.

Those who live Zen do not try to keep themselves sheltered from adversity and danger, but rather voluntarily expose themselves to it because it is the only way to progress. Even facing the challenges of Zen masters requires courage, because it undermines our certainties and the bonds to which we cling.

Starting from Sensitive Experience

Essential reality is not separate from the sensible world, but at the same time it is completely foreign to it. This is inconceivable to dualistic thinking.

Zen relies on sensible experience, taking it as a sure reference to anchor itself in reality; but sensible experience is the starting point for getting to know being, in which sensible phenomena occur and from which they are generated.

A good basis for avoiding being sidetracked by the mind is to stick to sensible reality in the immediacy of its appearance, in which one knows directly whether something is cold or hot, black or white, and there is no room for intellectual judgments.

Being is the foundation of the sensible world, and the sensible world is the basis for arriving at being. If one seeks truth without having acquired, thanks to the sensible world, a sense of reality, one wanders uselessly in imagination. If, on the other hand, one stops at the experience of the senses and mental products, one remains confined to a world of shadows, devoid of life. Therefore, it is important to remember that truth is not something static and stand-alone, but is something that is dynamically experienced and created from time to time in confrontation with the experience of the sensory world.

"A monk asked Yun Men, 'What is the Pure Buddha Body?' Yun Men replied, 'An enclosure around a flower garden.'" (The Blue Cliff Record).

He who dwells in being is no longer conditioned by the circumstances in which he finds himself living. The characteristics and adversities of the physical world have no power over him, because he has ceased to resist and oppose them.

To overcome the physical world, one must not try to avoid it, but rather must look closely at it, become intimate with it to the point of losing oneself in it.

"The monk said, 'What is the place where there is no heat or cold?' Tung Shan said, 'When it is hot, let the heat kill you; when it is cold, let the cold kill you.'" (The Blue Cliff Record).

The Illusory Value of Ideals

Men have a high regard for ideals; ideals are commonly held to be what is noblest that can dwell in the human soul, something to be cultivated and inspired by so that one's life has meaning and is beneficial to others.

But, in reality, ideals are only concepts, they are a product of the mind and, the higher they seem, the more tightly they lock us up in the prison of the mind.

Even in the search for ultimate reality there is a danger that, instead of possessing a real understanding of Zen, one is just following *concepts about* Zen, ideals about truth.

Concepts about Zen truths can be used without causing harm only by those who have already freed themselves from all concepts, and mainly from that of considering themselves individual subjects. Those who remain bound to the world of concepts, no matter whether they are trivial concepts or high ideals, can never, thanks to concepts, "jump" beyond the world of appearance.

"No monk in the world can jump out." (The Blue Cliff Record).

Time

There is no past, no future-not even a present: reality is *outside* of time.

"Yun Men said, 'I don't question you about the days before the fifteenth of the month; try to say something about after the fifteenth day.' Yun Men himself answered for everyone, 'Every day is a good day.'" (The Blue Cliff Record).

To look at one's memories as a real reference is to attribute reality to the past, and thus to be trapped in temporal categories, created by the mind.

There is no truth in the past, just as there is none in the future. And even the present, if understood as an intermediate location between a past and a future, is an illusion.

The only way to stay on the ground of reality is to rely on the timeless instant we are experiencing, an instant that comes from no "past" and is directed toward no "future." This timeless instant is the one in which we experience our awareness of being, and in which we concretely and directly know reality.

In the timeless instant, we know that time is an illusion, and that all the events of world history, which we previously believed to have succeeded one another, have actually been present in being simultaneously forever.

The mind induces us to believe that we can extend our gaze into an imaginary reality, remembering the past and speculating about the future; but each time we do so, we are only reaching even deeper into the prison of the mind.

"They only know how it was and how it would become: how can they realize that the swan is white and the raven is black?" (The Blue Cliff Record).

When we recognize its illusoriness, time ceases to be a limitation that constrains us, and becomes a means of expressing the freedom of being.

"Someone asked, 'During each of the twenty-four hours of the day, how should I apply the mind?' Chao Chou replied, 'You are used by the hours, I use them. What is this 'time' of which you speak?'" (The Sayings of Chao Chou).

Space

Even referring to the phenomena of the sensible world, Zen masters could take their cues from it to guide their students to an understanding of being, in which multiplicity and distances do not exist.

"The layman pointed to the snow in the air and said, 'Beautiful snowflakes-they don't fall anywhere.'" (The Blue Cliff Record).

Zen invites us to go beyond the common way of conceiving space. According to the common conception, to know a place means to be physically present, at a given time, in that specific place, and not in others. According to Zen, to know a place means to know them all, and not to know a place means to know none.

Zen requires that, in whatever place one is, one delves into it to the point of recognizing its deep essence, which resides in being, outside of space and time.

Unlike the ordinary man, one who lives Zen will not see in the physical world objects external to himself, which show the weight of years and whose nature remains obscure to him. For the person who lives Zen, objects will always be new and fresh, and he will hear his own voice in them, because they will express the message of being.

"Yang Shan asked a monk, 'Where are you from?' The monk replied, 'From Mount Lu.' Yang Shan asked, 'Have you visited the Peak of the Five Elders?' The monk replied, 'I have not been there.' Yang Shan said, 'Then you have not visited Mount Lu either.'" (The Blue Cliff Record).

Beauty of Nature and Attachment

It is considered normal to have preferences, including with regard to natural environments and various manifestations of nature. It seems obvious to prefer those environments and situations that by their beauty and poetry inspire feelings of peace and joy.

Yet this, too, is a subtle deception of the mind. There is nothing in nature and in the world that is not a manifestation of being and that does not reflect the perfection of being. If we are unable to feel wonder and admiration for any element of reality we come in contact with, it means that we are not open to the truth of being, but are locked up in the world of appearance, created and governed by the dualism of mind. Any object and any happening, no matter how insignificant and lowly it may seem, is a glow of being, is a full manifestation of truth.

Nothing and no one needs to become better than what it is.

"The earth hath not a speck of dust: what man hath not his eyes open?" (The Blue Cliff Record).

We Know the World by Creating It

Ordinary man attributes centrality to the sensible phenomena of the external world and the causal and space-time laws that seem to govern it. Zen, on the other hand, guides us to regain our centrality. We need to recognize in ourselves the foundation of being and the origin of the whole phenomenal world. Those who are able to do this, precisely by listening to and immersing themselves in the sensible world discover that reality cannot be grasped by the reductive concepts of dualistic thinking.

"He walks on a sheet of ice and runs on the blade of a sword. Sitting in the midst of the compounds of sound and form, he rises above them." (The Blue Cliff Record).

In the cognitive process, starting from the observation of the sensible world is the necessary first step to anchoring oneself in reality. But we cannot simply turn to the outside world, allowing ourselves to become entangled in the spectacle of ever-changing ephemeral phenomena. It is necessary to realize our contribution to the cognitive process, that is, the fact that everything we observe outside could not exist without our cognitive act.

If we can observe what is happening within us, and discover our true nature, we thereby open the way to being, to the One.

"If there were no men in the world, the manifold things would not exist [...]. All the manifold things are in our minds." (Hui Neng: Platform Sutra).

Denying All Representations of the Mind

To go beyond all concepts and representations of the mind, one must radically deny everything the mind can present as real: objects, consciousness, Buddha himself..

"Nan Ch'uan said, 'It is not the mind; it is not the Buddha; it is not the things.'" (The Door Without a Door).

Ordinary Man Is Already Perfect

God is not separate from the sensible world and ordinary man: ordinary man is already enlightened, and the world is already the perfect expression of the divine.

"With the blue sky and the bright day, there is no searching here and there!" (The door without a door).

"The Mind is not different from the Buddha, and the Buddha is not different from sentient beings." (Huang Po: Treatise on the Transmission of Mind).

Awakening from the Dream

Normally, because of the filters of the mind, humans see the world as in a mirror. Zen invites us to look at the world *directly*, finally entering into its life. In every aspect of the world pulses a life that is the life of being and that is our life.

It should be recognized that the world is not something outside of us: the world is us, we create it and enliven it. In the world we see the infinite faces of ourselves, in the world we hear the intimate voice of our heart.

The dominance of the mind robs us of the possibility of opening ourselves to being, and locks us into a dream world, consisting of separate, finite and lifeless elements.

"Nan Ch'uan pointed to a flower in the garden; he turned to the official and said, 'People today see this flower as if in a dream.'" (The Blue Cliff Record).

Filled with Being

By removing ourselves from the dominance of the mind, and stopping identifying with certain physical and psychological characteristics, we regain the freedom that belongs to our true nature. In this condition, we can no longer suffer any deprivation, because there is no longer anything that we are not. When we are nothing, in fact, everything comes to us, filling us up.

"A monk asked Yun Men, 'What is samadhi of each individual cell?' Yun Men replied, 'Rice in the bowl, water in the bucket.'" (The Blue Cliff Record).

Zen Must Not Be Reduced into Concepts

An ever lurking danger is that of *conceptually* understanding the truth of Zen. When we translate Zen's message into concepts, we have already lost it and fallen back into the dualistic mind (even if the concepts are about, for example, non-dualism and the need to transcend rationality).

To know Zen, one must escape the trap of *understanding* Zen. If we think we have come to have a clear idea of some teachings of Zen, then we have fallen into the dead world of concepts, and the living essence of Zen has eluded us.

We need to go beyond the concepts themselves of the Zen tradition. For example, Zen invites us to discover our fundamental nature; but our true nature is not something we can recognize and identify once and for all: we know our true nature to the extent that we experience its limitless freedom, which has no forms or characteristics in which it can be fixed.

Similarly, one cannot know the one who attains enlightenment, because enlightenment involves precisely the overcoming of all individual characteristics.

"I don't know who goes into the blue dragon cave." (The Blue Cliff Record).

Acknowledging the Miracle of Being

The world, as it is commonly perceived, appears to have stability and continuity. The objects we see appear solid, with a well-defined and fixed shape. But this apparent stability is only the work of the mind. In reality, each object of experience is an instantaneous appearance, and in each moment it appears unique and new in the miracle of being.

We cannot avoid following the indications of the senses and thought, but we must understand that the senses and thought do not have their foundation in themselves: they spring from being and are manifestations of being.

One who has understood Zen "loses his eyes," in the sense that he no longer sees the world as everyone else sees it, and he no longer deludes himself that he can enclose reality in the narrow patterns of thought: he acknowledges reality no longer through the indications of the senses and thought, but directly in its very essence.

"Even if one knows deeply the most abstruse doctrines, this is like a hair in a huge space. Even if one knows all the secrets of the world, it is like a drop of water in the great ocean." (The Door Without a Door).

Change Is Only Apparent

The changes we see happening in the world are a projection of the agitation of our minds.

"The mind operates all actions and the body perceives all evils; do not blame others for something that is actually within you." (Yung-Chia Ta-Shih: Song of Enlightenment).

At a deeper level, however, even the agitation of our mind is only apparent: in the essential reality of the One, there is no movement, and there is no need for anything to happen, because everything is already forever complete and perfect.

"Shih-t'ou said, 'The three worlds of desire, form and non-form, and the six paths of existence are only manifestations of your own mind. They are like the moon reflected in water or images in a mirror. How is it possible to consider them born or destined to die?'" (Lamp Transmission).

Stop

Zen teaching aims to stop men. In fact, Zen wants to stop the wandering of the mind, wants to stop the habit of relying on the judgments of the mind and considering oneself as individuals.

Zen wants to stop the dream state in which men spend their lives, to awaken them to reality.

If one abandons the illusion of time and individual existence, one discovers that one's reality is infinitely greater than one thought one had.

It is not a matter of meditating to reach a tranquil and ecstatic state of consciousness, for then one would still be in the deception of the self. To realize one's true nature one must experience, in an instant, eternity, freedom from time, and avoid identifying oneself with the activities of the ego.

"Don't move! If you move, thirty shots!" (The Blue Cliff Record).

Daily Commitment

In Zen, there is no line drawn between what is "earthly" and what is "spiritual." The light that a man brings into the world with his life does not die with his body, and it is of greater value the more that man's life has reflected the truth of being.

The concrete activity of men is the realization of being; and being is not to be sought in some "metaphysical heaven," but in the concreteness of one's daily endeavor. Only through strenuous earthly work can one come to experience, in being, dominion over heaven and earth.

For Zen, engagement in earthly life is therefore essential, and is the way to experience that which transcends earthly life.

True Zen

In Zen, the attainment of enlightenment is sometimes described with the image of a fish that, being able to swim up rapids, turns into a dragon. Indeed, in order to access fundamental truth, one must proceed against the current of the common mentality and the categories of the mind.

But the danger of mistaking as Zen knowledge what is only a mental construction should always be stressed. One can indeed go so far as to convince oneself of the validity of non-dualism and claim that it is the correct explanation of reality- but this would only be philosophy, it would only be a mental understanding, and it would not be Zen knowledge at all.

True Zen does not prefigure a gradual path punctuated by rewards and punishments, and it does not promise a final attainment tied to compliance with certain conditions.

When in a teaching we find no points of reference, no techniques to adopt, no attractive concepts about truth, and in general when we find nothing from which the self can feel reassured, encouraged and gratified--it is likely that we are dealing with a good teaching.

Alone or in Community

In Zen there is room for both solitary life paths and community organizations. Community living is more exposed to the risk of contaminating the message of Zen, because organizational needs often involve recourse to the modes of dualistic thinking; nevertheless, organized communities can be invaluable in providing the conditions and support to help people find the Way.

In any case, even if Zen is experienced within a community, it is always based on an enlightenment that each person realizes within himself, in a unique and unrepeatable way.

"The pure wind of immense spaces I alone know." (The Blue Cliff Record).

Zen Community

A Zen community is meant to be a bright spot for those who want to devote themselves to the search for truth.

The search for truth is not to be understood as a spasmodic chase after information, techniques, doctrines, places or situations, but rather as a patient listening, waiting to be able to hear the delicate and subtle message that is contained in the world we experience.

"Within heaven and earth, in space and time, there is a jewel, hidden in the mountain of form." (The Blue Cliff Record).

Truth, however, cannot be communicated to us, because it is something that concerns us intimately, and that only we can know.

"Only you can see them: white flowers, in the moonlight." (The Blue Cliff Record).

Subject and Object

In the reality of being, the distinction of subject and object is meaningless. In everything that experience presents us we find ourselves; and it is only in the immense vastness of the universe that we can recognize an adequate representation of ourselves.

"The subject finds peace when the object ends, the object ends when the subject finds peace. In the one emptiness the two are not distinct." (Seng-ts'an: Poem of Deep Faith).

When we no longer identify with a particular individuality, the supposed responsibility for our past actions also vanishes. Indeed, we no longer have the illusion that it is "we" who perform actions, and we know that everything happens by the free play of being.

"When one comes to Reality, one sees that it is devoid of both the self and the many forms of objectivity; and all the negative consequences of one's actions are instantly erased." (Yung-Chia Ta-Shih: Song of Enlightenment).

Sacredness Is Everywhere

There are no practices or objects more sacred than others. Therefore, one should not rely on the supposed "sacredness" of objects, practices or ways of transmitting truth.

Everything is of equal importance, and truth cannot be "transmitted" because we are already immersed in it. It is only necessary for each person, with an inner motion, to awaken.

Listening with the Eyes

Those who experience Zen do not deny multiplicity, nor do they seek to avoid the sensible world; indeed, sensible perceptions can even be the cue for realizing enlightenment. However, sensible perceptions do not constitute an independent foundation for knowledge: they themselves must find foundation in something else, namely in the mystery of being, from which they spring and in which they occur.

Zen refers to an entirely different kind of knowledge from that based on the senses: one must "listen with one's eyes" to the message of being, which emanates from every object, that is, one must "see" the world directly, without the mediation of the senses. Perception actually does not occur (as the mind would have us believe) through the senses, but within the mystery of being.

"When you perceive a sound, is it the sound that reaches the ear or is it the ear that goes to the sound? If both sound and silence are extinguished, what do you realize? If you listen with your ears, you cannot realize it. But when you listen with your eye, then it becomes intimately clear to you." (The Door Without a Door).

The Impossible Challenge

Zen realization requires absolute commitment and unlimited dedication, because in the eyes of common thinking Zen proposes an impossible and "deadly" challenge.

Those who have realized Zen experience each moment as "new," without the burden of a past and a future. But to achieve this one must stop clinging to beliefs dictated by the mind, accepting to put one's life at risk.

"If you want to hold the door and support the house, you must climb a mountain of swords with bare feet." (The door without a door).

Zen Is Not a Philosophy

Zen masters often tested their interlocutors by addressing seemingly paradoxical statements to them and urging them to respond with immediacy. If the interlocutor hesitated, and needed to stop and think, this clearly revealed their distance from Zen knowledge.

Those who experience Zen never have difficulty expressing the essence of reality, because its expression is not based on thought.

Zen should not be confused with a philosophy. To hold that because we are part of the unity of the whole, we are automatically already perfect and have nothing to seek is not Zen; it is only a conceptual shadow of the truth.

Zen truth is such insofar as it is experienced and insofar as it transforms one's perception of reality. If we have any doubt that our understanding of Zen is only mental, we can be sure that it is.

The Blows of the Masters

Zen masters tried to take advantage of every situation to flash the pupils' immediate understanding of reality. If the pupils, instead of turning to the unity of the whole, relapsed back into the distinctions and dualisms of the mind, it could happen that the master would strike them, to immediately stop the wandering of the mind and block the error.

"If you stop and think, it is as if you were sitting behind a black mountain while the bright sun shines in the sky, and the cool breeze blows over the earth." (The Blue Cliff Record).

To open access to the truth of being, pitting words against words is often counterproductive, while an immediate gesture can silence the mind's pretended knowledge.

Physical impact can elicit in the student a sudden contact with reality, awakening him from the dreams of imagination in which the mind was imprisoning him. And it is also an effective warning that Zen is not an intellectual pastime, but is about what maximally involves us, our flesh and more.

Some masters would immobilize the pupil almost preventing him from breathing, while simultaneously enjoining him to "speak": the purpose was to make him perceive that only when what one identifies with (the physical body, the concept of self as "person") is blocked and denied, is it possible to express something true, that is, coming from one's true nature.

When, by a master, a certain amount of violence removes the pupil's attachment to his own physical form, and the pupil recognizes that his own true nature is not subject to causal and space-time laws, all kinds of extraordinary actions become possible.

"The Great Spirit raised his hand and effortlessly separated the ten million layers of the Flower Mountain." (The Blue Cliff Record).

Advance and Retreat

Being free of the ego, Zen masters knew how to adapt to any situation, and with equal ease were available to both attack and surrender. In their dialogues with a student or with other masters, Zen masters had the ability to understand instantly, both the manifest side of an issue and its hidden implications (and this was called "grasping both the head and the tail of the tiger").

But that was not all. They, when clarification of the issue required their antagonist to have the last word, knew how to withdraw from the dispute, thus enabling the realization of a harmony of a higher level than the individual positions interpreted by the two interlocutors.

Many Schools, One Zen

There have been Zen masters who have developed teaching methods different from those of their school of origin. But this is not a problem at all in Zen, and indeed attests to the greatness of such masters.

Zen is perfectly compatible with a multiplicity of different schools and teachings; the superficial differences, due to the characteristics of the various masters and the intention to adapt the teaching to the pupils' abilities, are recomposed into a superior unity by the ability, which all true schools possess, to guide to the knowledge of being. The goodness of a school, in fact, does not depend on the ways it adopts, but on its grounding in knowledge that does not depend on the mind.

"South, North, East, West: let us return - And in the dead of night let us observe together the snow on the thousand peaks." (The Blue Cliff Record).

The Greatness of the Masters

The characteristic of the greatest Zen masters was that they never emphasized themselves. Even when they used abrupt words or gestures, they did not do so to elevate themselves, but always to promote true knowledge.

If a Zen master felt complacency about his own greatness, he would simply make a fool of himself-and show that he had no greatness.

Misunderstanding Teaching

Undoubtedly, even the teaching of great teachers can be misunderstood, and become for many an additional opportunity to race the mind and strengthen the sense of self. But this does not detract from the value of the teaching.

Those who can recognize the loftiness of a teaching will find in it a powerful call to walk the Way of true knowledge; others, will continue to roll uselessly on the steps of time.

The Language of the Masters

A Zen master uses language "lightly" (that is, without sinking into it), to convey content that, in itself, words and logical connections cannot include. He has the ability to use language without leaning completely on it, and thus without becoming entangled in the dualism of the mind and the "weeds" of arguments and judgments.

"Walking on the tip of the hundred weeds he shows the supreme reality." (The Blue Cliff Record).

The words of a Zen master contain more than just names and logical connections; what distinguishes them cannot be detected by analysis of the mind, and that is a "sense of truth," a resonance of ultimate reality.

What a Zen master seeks to convey with words is not found within words, and it is the experience of being.

Koans

One of the teaching methods of Zen is based on the use of koans. Koans contain sayings and anecdotes related to ancient masters, the meaning of which cannot be understood on the basis of the rational mind.

Working on a koan therefore involves seeking a type of understanding that does not refer to discriminating thinking.

The discursive mind labors in vain to elucidate the meaning of a koan, and when it finally, exhausted, gives up, space opens up for an understanding that comes from our deep nature, and that puts us in touch with being.

Our Real "Body"

We need to turn away from identification with our bodies, and the belief that we are the ones who act, move, and speak. It is in being that everything happens, and in it everything finds its origin.

When we come to recognize ourselves in being, we discover that our true body is beyond any size, and that our ability to communicate is beyond language and words.

"Master Sung-yuan asked, 'How come a man of great strength cannot lift a leg [to take a step]?' He also said, 'It is not with the tongue that we speak.'" (The door without a door).

"Raising one leg, I kick the Fragrant Ocean;
Lowering my head, I look down on the fourth sky of Dhyana.
There is no space big enough for this whole body.
Please write in your own words the last line." (The door without a door).

Every Product of the Mind Is Deceptive

To attribute reality to individual consciousness is to deceive ourselves; but we also deceive ourselves if we attribute reality to the Buddha, to the concept of God.

Truth is beyond both individual consciousness and the Buddha, it is beyond what we represent to ourselves as "earthly," and it is equally beyond what we represent to ourselves as "divine."

We need to be able to reject both the mind and all the concepts it creates, including concepts of the divine.

"A monk asked Ma-tsu, 'What is Buddha?' Ma-tsu replied, 'No mind, no Buddha!'" (The door without a door).

Don't Tell All

When, in order to teach truth, words are used, it is wise to stop before the topic is exhausted, limiting the words, and leaving room for understanding beyond the words.

"If you meet a swordsman, give him a sword; only if you meet a poet, offer him a poem. When you speak, provide only part of the explanation; do not provide the remaining part." (The door without a door).

Objects Are Better Than Concepts

The meaning of Zen is not to be sought in concepts. Every single object, in the concreteness and immediacy of its reality, validly represents the "meaning" of Zen, because in it being is directly manifested, and we can grasp it without getting lost in the illusion of concepts.

"A monk asked Chao Chou, 'What is the significance of Bodhidharma's coming from the West?' Chao Chou said, 'The oak tree in the garden.'" (The door without a door).

"Words cannot express things; language does not embody spirit. If you cling to words, you lose reality; if you stagnate in phrases, you remain in illusion." (The Door Without a Door).

Honesty in the Search

The basic condition for the search for truth is to be totally honest, first and foremost to oneself.

One must sincerely acknowledge one's ignorance, one's attachments, one's subjection to the dictates of the self. If we delude ourselves and convince ourselves that we have achieved some certainty, just because we can repeat some concepts learned from others, this fiction is making it impossible to be open to truth.

"Those who try to gain advantage lose the advantage." (The Blue Cliff Record).

Seeking One's Identity in Others

Ordinarily, each of us looks outside ourselves for our own meaning. Based on the feedback we get from others, we continually modify the image we have of ourselves.

Moreover, from others we also seek information and meanings, which we appropriate and with which we believe we reinforce ourselves. All this only exposes us to constant agitation, and the stability and balance to which we aspire are continually threatened.

We will never find externally the meaning and identity we seek. The answers are only within ourselves, where in the recognition of being we discover that our identity is that of the whole world.

Life Itself Is the Way

Even though one has had transcendent insight, it is easy to feel lost and not know how to proceed, as if there is neither direction nor solid ground for one's feet to stand on. But the solution is very simple. What life presents to us, moment by moment, is exactly our path; the situations we face in our daily lives are the steps that constitute our realization.

"Chao Chou was standing on a ladder when he saw Nan Ch'uan passing underneath. He hung on a rung, leaving his feet in the void, and shouted, 'Help! Help!' Nan Ch'uan climbed the ladder, saying, 'One, two, three, four, five.' Chao Chou said, 'Master, thank you for saving me.'" (The Sayings of Chao Chou).

Know Thyself

Above any Buddha, any master or religious tradition, one must place one's true nature.

"Master Wu-tsu said, 'Even Shakya and Maitreya are his servants. Now tell me: who is he?'" (The door without a door).

For those who have realized their true nature, life is a continuous gift. Everything that comes before his eyes conveys to him, in an infinity of different ways, the message of boundless love of being. He fears nothing because he is not an individual, therefore he possesses nothing and can lose nothing. But at the same time, everything that exists belongs to him and *is* himself.

For those, on the other hand, who have not realized their true nature, even what they think they possess will sooner or later be taken away from them, and will fade away as all illusions fade away.

"Master Pa-chiao said to the monks, 'If you have the staff, I will give it to you. If you do not have the staff, I will take it away from you!'" (The door without a door).

Inappropriate Eccentricities

Some people, having achieved significant achievements in Zen, tend to relate to others with behaviors that appear striking and bizarre, because they aim above all to give expression to the extraordinary nature of being. Such behaviors are inappropriate because they can only be understood by those who have already arrived at the same level of knowledge.

A wise master tries to adapt the manner of his teaching to the people he is addressing, so that they may maximally benefit from it. Those who do not act in this way are probably still subtly cultivating their own sense of self, their own need for supremacy.

Too Much Study

If the study of Zen remains only at the theoretical level, it is erroneous, and can easily increase egocentrism and conceit in those who cultivate it.

Undoubtedly, Zen masters, too, make use of words and concepts in their teaching; but in their case the conceptual level is used with an awareness of the limitations involved, and in order to create a bridge between higher knowledge and the level of the students.

Zen masters do not identify with words, and their teaching is about a reality beyond words.

"From the beginning, there is nothing hidden; I have never offered explanations." (The Blue Cliff Record).

Zen Knowledge

When perceptual data arise, Zen knowledge accommodates them with perfect transparency, without altering them with mental categories and individual inclinations.

But Zen knowledge above all knows how to grasp the dimension of being, in which there are no objects to be perceived.

He who knows beingness has recognized that his own individuality was only a deception, and having detached himself from it is no longer subject to the errors dictated by selfishness. He comes out of the realm of what is of value to most men, and for this they despise him. Even the deeds he has done in the past lose meaning and are no longer a part of him, like a dream that vanishes upon waking.

Fallout

Even those who are already advanced in their understanding of Zen can still make mistakes and stumble. For it is easy for him, although he has a good grasp of the essential reality, to tend to build upon it, believing he is explaining and highlighting it, arguments that cause him to fall back into conceptual thinking. And it is just as easy for him, observing his own ability to recognize the truth of being, to attribute that ability to himself, thus causing the sense of self and the belief that there is an individual cognitive activity to re-emerge.

Clearly, for a real understanding of Zen, it is necessary for the self to step aside.

"Ch'ang Ch'ing asked, 'What is the language of the Tathagata?' Pao Fu replied, 'Go drink tea.'" (The Blue Cliff Record).

Zen Should Always Be Regenerated

Zen masters, in their teaching, never passively repeat the gestures and words of their predecessors; they create new gestures and words, or use other masters' forms of expression in new ways, depending on the circumstances.

If Zen is not regenerated each time, its teaching becomes a hindrance to truth-seekers.

Truth Is Before Words

Those who, even in Zen, in order to learn the truth listen to the discourses of the masters (or the Buddha himself), have in a sense already lost sight of the truth.

We are accustomed to leaning on words, and to believing that we can better understand the meanings we seek if we can approach them by studying them through words. But the truth of Zen is not expressible in words, and the meaning of a speech must be understood before that speech is spoken.

Words, even when they come from those who have experience of being, are still something that overlaps with the immediacy and purity of reality, limiting and somewhat distorting it.

Certainly words can be helpful, not only in practical matters but also in teaching truth; however, it is good to use them with caution, always remembering that their one-sidedness and dualism can easily lead astray.

The Wisdom Beyond Consciousness

Ordinary knowledge, that of philosophies, that of the sciences-and even that of institutional religions-is based on the activity of consciousness, thus on discriminating thought and sensible perceptions.

The knowledge Zen refers to, on the other hand, is on a higher level, because it incorporates consciousness but is not limited to it. Zen reaches the level of being, of which consciousness is a manifestation.

If we dwell in being, we know that consciousness is part of it, but that it cannot come to know it, because being is beyond the dualistic limitations of consciousness.

Zen, like all currents of true wisdom, has the task of keeping contact with being alive, and those who experience Zen join the invisible chain of those who strive for the transmission of such supreme wisdom.

"Even if the sun turns cold and the moon hot, and despite all the strength of the wicked, true doctrine will always remain indestructible." (Yung-Chia Ta-Shih: Song of Enlightenment).

The Moral Equivocation

Moral action is not a cause of enlightenment, but rather a consequence of enlightenment.

It is not behavior that is considered altruistic that makes us better men; as long as we remain in the realm of discriminating consciousness, we are unable to perform actions that are truly free of selfishness.

Only if we free ourselves from the bonds of dualistic thinking do our actions become authentically moral.

"Both committing evil and practicing good stem from attachment to form." (Huang Po: Treatise on the Transmission of the Mind).

The Deepest Compassion

One who lives Zen is animated by a compassion infinitely superior to that commonly experienced; for he, having overcome the deception of the ego, does not see other people as separate from him, but as intimately connected and united with him.

He knows that his life is rooted and reflected in the lives of others, for in recognizing his true nature he has recognized that it is one with the true nature of all.

Using the Senses, but Not to Take Advantage of Them

Zen teaches not to seek gratification in the world of the senses.

The quiet acceptance of simple natural happenings is already cause for peace and satisfaction.

If we turn to the world of the senses without expectations, without superimposing on it the interpretations of the mind and the desires of the self, the world of the senses will open the way to a perception of reality that does not rely on the senses.

Do Not Start from the Assumption of Imperfection

When we begin our journey in search of truth, we necessarily start with the realization that our life lacks something fundamental, and we turn to teachings and practices that we believe can "cure" our malaise. But the distinction between something imperfect (material life) and something that has the ability to cure imperfection (the teachings and practices) is artificial and wrong.

The material world is itself the way to cure imperfection, and indeed is itself a manifestation of perfection.

If we then come to dwell in being, we realize that in it both problems and "cures" lose their meaning and disappear, along with the illusory world of which they were a part.

It is therefore better, in our search for truth, not to start out with a baggage of beliefs and not to direct our path on paths already marked out.

Even Zen traditions easily end up being more of a hindrance than a help: if we are free from ideological and moral conditioning, we discover that in the regions of being there already exists a free and welcoming path, which has always been open, just for us.

Backward Path

What characterizes the human being is consciousness, which is like a light by which we perceive the external world and our inner life. If, instead of following the normal flow of consciousness, which is always directed toward objects (inside or outside of us), we try to investigate consciousness itself, we do not find it, but we discover that there is something that is observing consciousness, and that is independent of it. This backward movement, aimed at going back to what is before consciousness, leads us to know our true nature.

"Riding an ox in reverse, entering the Buddha's shrine." (The Blue Cliff Record).

By that route, we learn to perceive the world independently of consciousness and the ordinary modes of the senses and thought: important as it is, consciousness must therefore also be overcome.

"A good thing is not as good as no thing." (The Blue Cliff Record).

No Attachment

If we rely on the discriminating mind, we continually develop judgments and preferences, and the measure of our subjection to conceptual thinking will be our level of attachment. The stronger the sense of being an individual subject, the stronger the attachment to anything that confirms that belief.

Knowledge of being goes hand in hand with our ability to let go of all attachments. Indeed, to be free from attachment, we must be able to see reality outside the dualisms of the mind, recognizing in each of its elements an expression of the One.

"The Buddha says that [the sands of the Ganges] can contain all kinds of treasure or perfume without feeling avarice; and they can be soiled by all kinds of filth, without feeling nauseated. Such an attitude is that of one who becomes free from mental attachment." (Huang Po: Treatise on the Transmission of the Mind).

"Attachment is always over the line, let it go, and things will go as they should go, while Being does not move or stand still." (Seng-ts'an: Poem of Deep Faith).

Letting go of attachment leads to the recognition that there is nothing to seek, because we are already complete and perfect, in being.

"To become free from mental attachment may take more or less time, but once this state is reached all practices and all knowledge come to an end; indeed nothing is achieved." (Huang Po: Treatise on the Transmission of the Mind).

Determinism and Freedom

Those who experience Zen "do not ignore," so to speak, the law of causality.

Knowing being does not make one immune to spatio-temporal determinism, but allows one to simultaneously experience the deep reality, which is the realm of freedom, and in which time as linear movement does not exist.

Causality and space-time laws arise within being as an apparent manifestation, whose insubstantial reality vanishes when we recognize its source.

So That Life Is Not Useless

If man does not come to dwell in being, he deprives himself of the realization of his true nature, which enables him to experience full and unlimited freedom.

"When the spiritual wheel turns, not even a master can keep up. It moves in all directions: above and below, south and north, east and west." (The Door Without a Door).

A life that does not come to know the truth of being is something unfinished and useless.

The False Teachers

Even in Zen, one must be able to recognize false teachers, that is, those who base their teaching on concepts. A rigorous cultural and moral commitment, however much it may lead to holding important positions, does not testify to any value regarding actual knowledge of Zen.

"Blinding the eye on the forehead, he adheres to the pointer of the scales. Throwing away body and life, a blind man leads other blind men." (The Door Without a Door).

Only the one who has overcome the illusion of causal and space-time patterns is a true master.

"He who sits on the top of a hundred-foot-high pole, even though he has entered the Way, is not yet realized. He must step forward from the top of the pole, and show his whole body into the world in ten directions." (The door without a door).

Enemies Are a Gift

Even those who cause harm to others are moving within being. He could not conceive any thought or move any muscle except through the harmony of being.

He who suffers evil may come to realize that that evil was exactly what he needed to overcome barriers that prevented him from accessing his true nature. He may then come to feel deep gratitude toward his enemies, for no evil suffered is remotely comparable to the joy of knowing being.

"Others may say ill of me and despise me, but their effort is useless, like that of one who tries to burn the sky with a flashlight [...]. They are actually my good friends: if, when I am despised, I feel neither enmity nor preference, there grows in me the love and humility that are generated from the unborn." (Yung-Chia Ta-Shih: Song of Enlightenment).

When Teachers Seem to Lean on the Sensitive World

The world is not composed of solid objects endowed with continuity, as the mind would have us believe, but of fleeting images that appear and disappear at every moment. Magnitudes, distances and temporal continuity are mental constructions that must be gotten rid of.

When, in his or her teaching, a master refers to sensible objects and material situations, he or she does so in order to create a "bridge" for people to approach the sphere of ultimate truth. If a master did not relate to the material world he would not introduce "errors" into his teaching, however, at the same time he would deny many people the opportunity to approach it.

In any case, every master spreads his teaching "without purpose," just as it is without purpose the blooming of flowers that no one will be able to see. It is an action performed because one's nature induces one to perform it, without setting oneself results, and aware of the freedom of being.

"In spring, for whom do the myriads of flowers bloom?" (The Blue Cliff Record).

Zen "Thieves"

In Zen, a true master is called a "thief." He in fact robs people of beliefs and certainties based on the ordinary way of thinking.

When a master asks for an opinion, one must be careful not to refer to scales of values and make judgments: in fact, the master wants precisely to invite the interlocutor to show that he can escape from the complications of thought, and instead use the answer to manifest the transcendent.

Outside and Inside

Zen's invitation to direct the search within oneself can be misunderstood. In fact, many believe that the "inside" consists of thoughts, consciousness, and cultivating meditation. For Zen, however, all this is still "outside."

That which refers to the self, to thinking, to acting to achieve results, to choosing what is best, is still infinitely distant from the intimacy of our true nature.

"Ma-tsu said, 'Escaping evil and sticking to positive things, meditating on the Void and entering the state of deep concentration-that is doing something. But those who chase after something external move away from Truth.'" (Sayings of the ancient personalities).

The Experience of Being

He who has understood his own true nature (which is not consciousness, but he who "sees" consciousness), does not fear death and has no attachments in life.

He intimately communes with everything that comes before him, and in every moment experiences eternity.

He knows that time is an illusion and that, in being, nothing is born and nothing dies, nothing changes or is lost, everything is as it should be, from ever and forever.

The experience of being is a life that blossoms from death, for it is only when one stops attributing reality to one's physical and psychological individuality that one can be born to true life.

"In a single moment of consciousness, we see the whole of eternity; eternity is exactly this very moment. If you understand the consciousness of this very moment, you understand the one who sees." (The Door Without a Door).

Riding the Tiger

In Zen there is no point in repeating gestures or words out of imitation, or to conform to tradition. Any action that does not express truth departs from it.

The Zen follower must always strive for maximum adherence to reality, without arbitrariness.

On the other hand, everything is becoming and in mutual correlation, nothing is fixed and independent of everything else, and the freedom of being is unlimited. It is therefore natural that those who experience Zen do not attach themselves to any object, situation or idea.

This ability to adapt to the living flow of reality is called "riding the tiger," and should not be confused with the attitude of those who, out of convenience and without real knowledge of being, adapt to circumstances in order to carry out their own project.

Blind

It is normal to call someone who does not know the truth "blind." But in Zen the same term is also used to refer to one who, being able to know being without the mediation of the senses and mind, no longer sees the world in the limited way of those who can perceive it only with their physical eyes.

Only Ourselves Can Free Ourselves

It is we ourselves who, by continually feeding the patterns and beliefs of the mind, build the walls that hold us captive. It is therefore impossible for anything from the outside to free us. From the outside we can receive suggestions, but then we must be the ones to use those suggestions to dismantle the castle of illusions we had built.

"One day, while all the monks were outside, Chao Chou shouted from the meditation hall, 'Fire! Fire!' When all the monks ran to the door of the meditation hall, Chao Chou closed the door, slamming it shut. The monks did not know what to do. But Nan Ch'uan threw the key through the window, and Chao Chou opened the door." (The Sayings of Chao Chou).

Meet Directly

To recognize a man who has understood Zen, one must be on the same plane as him, one must therefore be able to have direct contact with reality.

Direct contact with reality requires skipping the mediation of thought, and opening oneself immediately and intimately to what life presents to us, without cushioning its impact or seeking shelter behind mental filters.

"Meeting a man of the Way on the street, meet him neither with words nor with silence. A punch on the jaw: if you want to understand him, understand him directly!" (The Door Without a Door).

The Iron Yoke

It has been said that living Zen is like carrying an iron yoke. When we participate in the dimension of being, we become part of an incalculable force that dominates and directs our lives. We remain anchored in being, centered in ourselves, and can no longer lose ourselves whose paths of illusion. It is an indestructible bond, and its strength guarantees our freedom.

Fools Who Can See

To understand, at the conceptual level, the need to go beyond all conceptualizations is to remain still bound to the inconclusive activity of the mind.

To encounter truth, one must stop looking for answers at the level of the concepts. Only when one stops "understanding" does one begin to "see."

"Ch'an monks who can see do not understand." (The Blue Cliff Record).

The knowledge of those who live Zen is worthless in the eyes of the world, and it could not be otherwise.

For those who live in the Platonic cave, that is, in the prison of the discriminating mind, there is no other reality than that of the shadows cast on the cave wall.

Thought Is Not a Danger

Just as sensible data, when intimately experienced, reveal being, of which they are a manifestation, the same is true of thoughts.

It is only when we place the filter of the mind before direct knowledge of reality that thoughts form an illusory veil that obscures life. But in their concrete reality, thoughts are only phenomena that, like the phenomena of the external world, appear, subsist for some time, and then go away. If we do not attach ourselves to them, they do not cause any problems.

"Ma-tsu said, 'One thought happens to another without interruption, the previous one does not relate to the next, and each is calm and concluded in itself.'" (Sayings of the ancient personalities).

Birth and Death

Those who dwell in being know that there is nothing frightening in death, and that ultimately death does not exist.

That which we truly are is not born and does not die, has no boundaries or limitations, undergoes neither growth nor loss.

"If we attach ourselves to this objective world, birth and death appear, just as waves appear from water [...]. If we detach ourselves from this objective world, there is no birth and death, and we are like water that follows its course uninterruptedly." (Hui Neng: Platform Sutra).

Don't Look for What Is Already in You

We will not find truth if we search for it as we search for an object, that is, as something that, with definite and precise characteristics, exists outside of us. We must discover that truth is a living creative flow, and that we ourselves are its source.

"When one learns that Mind is transmitted from one Buddha to another, one imagines that Mind is a particular object, and one tries to understand it; but this means looking for something outside of Mind [...]. In reality there is only Mind. You cannot chase it with another Mind. [...] It is like someone looking for a gem, which is actually on his forehead; as long as he is looking for it outside himself, it is impossible for him to find it. When he discovers that the gem is on his forehead, the discovery has nothing to do with the efforts made to search for it outside. That is why the Buddha says, 'By obtaining my enlightenment I have achieved nothing.'" (Huang Po: Treatise on the Transmission of Mind).

To Cling to Being Is to Lose It

To dwell in being one must have overcome all desire, even that for being.

For those who have experienced enlightenment there is the subtle but very dangerous risk of wishing to stop at it. It is understandable that, once one has cast one's gaze on the free and serene world of being, one tends to cling to it, trying to hold on to the position obtained. But this is precisely the way to move away from enlightenment.

The desire to hold on to the condition of enlightenment comes from the ego; it is an extreme attempt by the ego to reassert itself.

Enlightenment is not bargainable, one cannot obtain it in exchange for something, and one cannot withhold it as one's own possession.

The correct attitude is to never stop at complacency about the knowledge one has attained, and to always open oneself up to life, stripped of any cognitive baggage and regardless of the advantages, comparisons and judgments of others. In this way one's proceeding will be the very proceeding of being, from enlightenment to enlightenment.

"With stick on his shoulders, regardless of others, he goes straight over the myriad peaks." (The Blue Cliff Record).

"In my school there are only two kinds of diseases. One is looking for a donkey while already riding on it. The other is not wanting to get off, having recognized that you are riding a donkey. [...] I say to you that you must not ride on the donkey: you are the donkey! The whole world is the donkey: how is it possible to ride it?" (Teachings of Master Fo-yen).

Empty Substantiality

With enlightenment the supposed objectivity of the world vanishes, and it is revealed that what the senses and mind perceive is actually emptiness, an

"empty substantiality." (The Blue Cliff Record).

The enlightened man therefore "does not see" the world; although his senses provide him with the same perceptions that other men have, he takes in these perceptions and lets them flow, without presupposing at their basis a world of objects that are solid and stable in their characteristics. This "unseeing" of the enlightened man is not something that can be recognized by others, for each man must develop this capacity from within. Enlightenment reveals that one's own essence, and the essence of the whole world is the result of an inner creative process. The essence of the world is therefore substantiated by freedom. In the vital creative act of being there can be no limits.

"The White Ox is pure, naked and clean in free space." (The Blue Cliff Record).

Not Only Knowledge

Understanding the patterns of the mind and not being fooled by its reductive filters is indispensable, but it is still only a partial realization of Zen. It is then necessary to know how to produce gestures and words that can bring out, beyond the illusory world of the mind, the real world of being.

If we stop halfway, we do not achieve true Zen, but only a sterile complacency about the understanding we think we possess.

Simultaneously

What, seen through the categories of the mind, seems to happen in different places or at different times, in the reality of the One happens simultaneously, and to the same subject.

There is not a single event in the universe that does not happen to us; and the various events, whether pleasant or painful, are experienced simultaneously and inseparably in the One.

"On the southern mountain the clouds gather, on the northern mountain it rains; [...] In suffering, happiness - In happiness, suffering." (The Blue Cliff Record).

Hit by the Arrow

Assimilating the superficial forms of Zen, imitating them and using them to delude ourselves that we have reached a higher level of spiritual understanding, holds us at the level of the conceptual mind, far from the cleanliness and sharpness of Zen.

"For those who play with a ball of mud, there will never be an end." (The Blue Cliff Record).

We must not linger in the games of the mind, but be quick to grasp the direct contact with reality. Reality launches its arrow at us in every moment, its call to meet it. If we know how to recognize the arrow and be struck by it, a new life will begin.

The Subtle Feeling

It is not through concepts and imagination that enlightenment can be known. If we *think* enlightenment, and if we strive and strive to attain it, we deepen the groove that separates our heaviness and coarseness from the lightness and fineness of enlightenment.

Enlightenment does not depend on the mind and senses, but can occur at a material experience. In that case, we experience a sensation that is more subtle than ordinary sense experiences, and we perceive the life and language of an object, and of every object. We discover that every object, which we previously thought of as "inanimate," is actually animated by a pulsating life and, by its being what it is, expresses a message, nonverbal but symbolic, which is the message of being. In that message we recognize ourselves, and we recognize the eternal unity of the whole.

"In ancient times there were sixteen bodhisattvas. When it was time for the monks' bath, the bodhisattvas set about washing. Suddenly they experienced awakening to the fundamental nature of water. All of you, worthy students of Ch'an, how do you understand what they said, 'Subtle feeling reveals enlightenment, and we have attained buddhahood'? To understand this you must make your perception extremely subtle and acute." (The Blue Cliff Record).

Don't Look for a "Cake"

If we devote ourselves to Zen in order to seek answers, knowledge, fulfillment, security, peace or whatever else we miss or find desirable, we are still pursuing the aims of the ego.

If we imagine that in the "transcendent" we will find satisfactions superior in quantity and quality to those we have experienced in the sensible world, we are binding ourselves even more to the patterns of the mind.

For awakening to take place there must be, not an increase in knowledge, but a loss of knowledge; there must be enactment not of a strengthening of self, but an abandonment of the sense of ego.

"A monk asked Yun Men, 'What is the teaching beyond the Buddhas and Patriarchs?' Yun Men said, 'Cake.'" (The Blue Cliff Record).

Understanding the Precepts

Throughout history, Buddhist teaching has also been translated into a series of precepts. Moral rules and precepts show men certain actions, which flow from direct knowledge of ultimate reality; the purpose is to foster, in men who will in turn repeat such actions, insight into the profound vision that inspired them.

Unfortunately, however, the precepts are generally understood as valid in themselves, and end up feeding a "moralistic" conception of the religious message.

To perform altruistic actions, or in praise of the divine, is still to remain tied to the judgments of the mind, to its distinguishing between "good" and "evil" on the basis of its reductive and one-sided view. It is therefore not by the fulfillment of precepts received from outside that one comes to know being, but only by an initiative that starts from the depths of oneself. The fulfillment of precepts,

"is to push down the head of an ox to induce it to eat." (The Blue Cliff Record).

The Role of the Master

A Zen master does not pass on any knowledge to his students; he does not bring his students the "nourishment" of some doctrine or some secret wisdom. Zen truth is not, in fact, something pre-established that can be described and handed down.

Zen truth must be created and experienced by each person individually, moment by moment. To this end, a Zen master can identify, and help remove, the attachments that prevent students from resting in their true nature.

When the pupil has brought valid inner work to maturity, the Zen master can provide him, by appropriate intervention, with the cue to finally tear open the veil of appearance and see reality directly. But one must avoid understanding this cooperation between master and pupil as mechanical and describable in conceptual terms.

"All the monks in the world describe it in vain." (The Blue Cliff Record).

For the master-pupil relationship to bear fruit, it is necessary for both to have abandoned identification with an individual role and personality. So the pupil must not *think* that the master will hand him a solution from the outside that will save him, and the master must not *think* that the pupil is someone who needs his help to save himself.

"The Way has no back roads; those who travel it are lonely and dangerous." (The Blue Cliff Record).

New Paths

Those who live Zen are always able to create original actions and expressions that break the patterns and shed new light on the world.

On the other hand, those who cannot break out of the dualistic mindset will continue to repeat old patterns and common concepts.

"Two by two, three by three, they walk the old road." (The Blue Cliff Record).

From Great Distances

Often the questions Zen masters ask their students are like eagles soaring from great distances.

The masters want to offer students an opportunity to demonstrate their understanding of Zen, and they launch their questions from the great distances of the dimension of being.

In order to answer them, learners must be able to see far beyond the data of the senses and the mind.

Finite and Infinite

If we want to say a word about truth, it cannot be our self that speaks. For truth to be able to express itself, the self must first have withdrawn.

The sensible and transcendent levels are mutually exclusive: for one to emerge, the other must be extinguished.

While in the sensitive level positive experiences are always destined to end, in the transcendent level there is no end to the eternal shining of the light of being.

"On the Ten Lands spring has come to an end and the flowers wither - On the coral forest the sun is eternally radiant." (The Blue Cliff Record).

Enlightenment Has No Cause

When one tries to reconstruct and retrace the steps that seem to have led to enlightenment, one is turning one's eyes toward something dead, something that is no longer real and will therefore lead one astray on the terrain of illusion.

Enlightenment is to be grasped instantaneously; if you plan to approach enlightenment by a gradual path, you will only encounter endless difficulties and complications.

It is a matter of realizing that our true nature is beyond the causal, spatial and temporal limits generated by the mind.

"A man of valor is prior to the mind, heaven and earth not yet separated." (The Blue Cliff Record).

From Slaves to Lords

The transformation that takes place with enlightenment is something very concrete; it is not simply a change of perspective in the way we see the world; what takes place is an actual change of self and the world.

Before enlightenment, we are irrelevant individuals subjected to the conditions of a foreign and often hostile world.

After enlightenment, there are no more separations or limits to one's freedom. If we were previously subject to the laws of the physical world, we are now its lords and creators.

Rebirth

The attainment of truth does not occur by a slow and gradual path in the world of time and space; it occurs in a leap outside time and space; and what, in time and space, seems to have preceded the event of awakening is not recognized as the path that led to that event. The man who walked a certain path before awakening is not the same man who achieved awakening.

The awakened man can no longer recognize himself as what he thought he was before awakening, because he knows that that image he had of himself was vain and deceptive, the product of his own mind and the way the minds of others saw him.

The End of the Search

With enlightenment, the deep nature of reality, of which we were already a participant all along, now becomes manifest.

Becoming aware of our true nature and spreading Zen knowledge does not increase the truth in the world, because it is already eternally fulfilled and perfect:

"Raising the flag of Teaching and establishing the essential meaning is like scattering flowers on brocade." (The Blue Cliff Record).

With enlightenment, however, the search comes to an end; the subtle anxiety due to the feeling that we are missing something ends, and a deep peace takes its place.

Enlightenment cannot be seen in the characteristics with which man appears in the sense world, because his nature is different from and incompatible with the sense world.

Before the World Appears

To induce students to get rid of the complications of the mind, an ancient master explained Zen by simply raising a finger. In every smallest element of reality is present the whole; moreover, Zen invites us to recognize the whole even *before* some element of reality shows itself.

"When one speck of dust moves, it is the whole universe that moves; one flower blooms, and it is the whole world that opens. But before the speck of dust moves, and before the flower blooms, in what way will you be able to see it?" (The Blue Cliff Record).

The more we orient ourselves to simplicity, the closer we are to the mystery of being. It is therefore necessary to loosen all ties, including those with the Teaching, with the search for enlightenment and with the Buddha himself.

Enlightenment is not the result of a path: it is a miracle, an "impossible" event according to the categories of the mind, and it occurs without a cause and without merit, in total freedom.

No One Can Become Enlightened

One cannot *become* enlightened, because one cannot become what one already is. To look at enlightenment as a future goal, and to adopt practices to achieve it, is to still be imprisoned in conceptual thinking. But enlightenment cannot be *understood*; it implies that one knows how to escape the filter of thought.

It is not the self that becomes enlightened; it is not the individual who, by improving himself, attains enlightenment. Enlightenment has nothing to do with the person, and as long as you remain within the scope of the person you are completely excluded from enlightenment.

Compass

The north star of truth seekers must be immediacy, closeness, intimacy.

How do we recognize truth?

[[It is] "like meeting one's father at a crossroads. There is no need to ask others whether it is him or not." (The Door Without a Door).

The Destination

About being nothing can be said; yet, in one's inner self, everyone knows what it is.

"Where Being and every awakened man are not separated, there words cannot reach, for this place is not of the past, nor of the present, nor of the future." (Seng-ts'an: Poem of Deep Faith).

"The inside and the outside will become one, in a natural way. Then you will be like a mute man who has had a dream: you alone will know him, within you .[...] On the brink between life and death, you will enjoy perfect freedom. In the six realms and four modes of existence, you will live joyfully in innocence." (The Door Without a Door).

Printed in Great Britain
by Amazon